Little Soph
and
Lanky Flop

Little Sophie and Lanky Flop

ELS PELGROM
wrote the Dutch words

Arnold Pomerans
put them into English

THE TJONG KHING
drew the pictures

FARRAR STRAUS GIROUX
NEW YORK

Library of Congress catalog card number: 87-45752
Published in The Netherlands as *Kleine Sofie en Lange Wapper*
by Em. Querido's Uitgeverij B.V.
First published in Great Britain by Jonathan Cape Ltd.
Printed in the United States of America
First American edition, 1988

Contents

Little Sophie was always very curious about things. It wasn't that she pried. It wasn't that at all. She just liked to know about things, to find out about everything that went on in the world outside.

Her father and mother were often at their wits' end –

"Where does water come from?"

"Yes, but before it got into the tap?"

"Can a mosquito put your blood back again through your skin?"

"Do birds ever go outside the earth's atmosphere?"

– she asked all sorts of questions that were difficult to answer.

Because Sophie had been ill for a very long time and the doctor had ordered her to stay in bed, a teacher used to come and visit her at home. His name was Mr Jerome; he had friendly blue eyes and tufts of hair round his mouth. At times Sophie drove the poor man to distraction.

"Mr Jerome, why is grass green?"

"That, Sophie, is because . . ." and Mr Jerome talked for a good hour about oxygen, about ozone and nitrogen, and about aphids with their green protective colouring. "Did you follow all that?" he asked at the end when he felt he had said everything that had the slightest bearing on the subject.

"Yes. But why is grass green?" asked Sophie.

"Heavens above!" Mr Jerome threw his arms up in despair. "Look, child, you mustn't ask questions like that. It's because the good Lord arranged things that way!"

Sophie was well aware that Mr Jerome didn't believe this at all. She pressed her lips tight shut, picked up her rag doll Lanky Flop, and disappeared almost completely under the bedclothes.

"What exactly happens to you when you're dead?" she asked.

"I'm not going to answer any more stupid questions," said Mr Jerome and ran out of the room.

The Dolls' Theatre

That evening Sophie's father and mother had been asked to go to a party. Mr Jerome came for supper because he was going to baby-sit.

Now, Mr Jerome was a poor man, an out-of-work teacher. The meal that night was the best he had had for six months and on top of that he drank three glasses of red wine. After supper, as soon as Sophie's parents had left, he settled down in a deep armchair, turned on the television and fell asleep. He slept and slept and never moved, not even when the clock struck twelve.

At that moment Sophie was lying in her bed, wide awake. She had tried everything: counting sheep, and fleecy clouds, and listening to the ticking of the clock – nothing had helped. There was a night light in her room but Sophie kept her eyes tightly shut.

Terror, the fat tomcat, lay at her feet. He was awake, too, looking about through eyes narrowed to slits.

Suddenly Sophie heard a soft shuffling sound. And then something rustled. Little feet seemed to be tripping across the floor, although they must be very little feet indeed, since they could hardly be heard on the thick carpet. The noises were coming from every corner of the room. And there were also some slow, muffled footsteps.

Then there was a thud, a very soft kind of thud. A door had been opened, creaking and squeaking. Another thud: the door had been shut. It must be a tiny door, one made of paper or cardboard.

Sophie didn't move. She lay there, straining her ears and listening. Then she heard whispering.

"Stop it! Stop it!" somebody said angrily. And: "Ow! Hell and damnation! Why don't you look where you're going?"

"Shhh! Stop making such a row!"

"What the hell do I care? As if anyone ever damn-well stirred around here!"

Sophie had never in her life heard so much bad language. She raised her eyebrows and listened hard.

The grumbling and the clattering about came closer. She heard the hurrying footsteps again, and then the rustling of silk. There was a noise that sounded like the scraping of chairs or benches.

The big clock struck a quarter past twelve. Everything grew still. But that didn't last long.

Something was moving in Sophie's high bed. First one leg was pushed out from under the pillow, and then another leg. It was Lanky Flop. He sat up straight, stretched, gave a big yawn and scratched his ear. Carefully Sophie turned her head to look. Lanky Flop crawled over to the side of the bed and let his long legs dangle down.

Sophie peered out into the room. Although the light was dim she could see everything perfectly well. The biggest surprise was that she wasn't frightened by what she saw.

All her dolls and animals had come out of their boxes and drawers; they had arranged little chairs and stools in three rows and were now sitting on them, waiting. In one corner of the room stood her little theatre. The curtains were twitching and just then a tail stuck out through a chink. The dolls and the animals began to laugh. Someone called out: "Come on, let's get on with it! Up with the curtain!"

But somebody's hand or paw was holding the curtains tightly closed and nothing happened.

The audience grew impatient. They all sat there, talking to each other, rustling paper bags and passing fruit drops and chocolates along the rows. Teddy Bear was examining the plaster scrollwork on the ceiling through his opera glasses. The giraffe had a choking fit and those sitting behind him slapped him on his back and neck. Someone threw a little tin of cough lozenges across to him. Then a bell rang.

"Shhh! Be quiet! They're going to start. It's beginning!" could be heard from all sides.

August the Clown, with his big round nose, came to the front of the stage and beat on a drum.

"Ladies and gentlemen!" he said. "Honoured guests! Your patience will be rewarded. You are about to see a play called *The World is a Vale of Tears*, in four acts. Please pay careful attention – it is an educational play."

"Boo! Boo!" the audience called out. "We don't want to be educated, we want to laugh!"

August the Clown pretended he hadn't heard. Turning round he shouted: "For goodness' sake, isn't that lazy nincompoop of a Punch ready yet? Come on, Punch, what's keeping you? Are you still dressing up?"

"All right, all right, I'm coming!" someone called from behind the stage.

The curtains went up and there stood Mr Punch, wearing nothing but a long shirt and a nightcap on his head. In one corner of the stage was a gallows, with the hangman standing next to it. A policeman and Judy had stuck their heads out from the wings and were looking curiously at the rows of spectators.

Sophie sat up straight in bed. Round-eyed she stared at everything that was going on in her room. There were two red spots on her cheeks, from her fever and the excitement.

Judy stepped forward. She had a baby in her arms, screaming its head off. Judy herself was crying and screaming. And the audience screamed loudest of all.

"Punch and Judy! Punch and Judy!" they shouted. "We're sick of Punch and Judy! We want something new for a change. That old stuff will send us all to sleep!"

Something whizzed through the air and clattered at August the Clown's feet: a silver dagger, studded with "precious stones" made of glass.

"That was meant for you!" called the dachshund, who was sitting in the front row. "And don't run away with the idea I don't know how to aim. That was just a warning."

His girlfriend, the black poodle, pouted: "It's a disgrace, that's what it is, an absolute disgrace. Punch and Judy's only good enough for fools. We want something we can get our teeth into!"

The audience grew noisier and noisier. Some even stood on their chairs and waved their fists in the air. But the dachshund and the poodle were having a hard time since the pig, the seal and the rocking toy behind them began to pummel them, raining blows on them and shouting: "Show-offs! We want to laugh, we want to laugh!"

"Yes, yes, we want to laugh!" the others joined in.

Judy's baby screamed louder and louder and Judy herself became so confused by all the turmoil that she flung her yelping child right into the middle of the excited audience. There was a roar of laughter and the poor child was thrown from one spectator to the next, until it reached the last row, where it rolled into a dark corner and lay still.

The hangman wanted to carry on with the play. He set off after Punch, but Punch had seen a way of escaping the noose. He clambered up a table leg and hid on the window-sill. The policeman and the hangman hunted for him everywhere.

And August the Clown, speechless with dismay, threw up his arms.

Suddenly everything went quiet. At first Sophie couldn't make out what had happened, but then she saw that all the dolls and all the animals had turned round and were looking at her bed. But not at her. They were looking at Terror.

Terror had stood up, stretching his legs and arching his back. Slowly and deliberately he jumped off the bed, crossed the room to the stage and climbed up on to it. Then he sat down and wrapped his tail carefully round his legs.

"You want to see something you can get your teeth into, do you, something serious?" he said. "Well, so you shall. By coincidence, I happen to have written a very difficult play. Shall we have a look at it?"

"What's it called?" somebody shouted.

"It doesn't matter what it's called," said Terror. "I don't actually know myself. It's a long play and it deals with What Life Has to Offer. Would you like to see it?"

"Yes, yes! What fun!"

"It has nothing whatever to do with fun," said Terror crossly. "There are human beings in my play, too, human beings who can talk. You know, just like in fairy tales. But this is no fairy tale. You'll see!"

Terror gave August the Clown a sign and he, together with Death, dragged on to the stage a couple of long poles round which something had been wrapped. They each went to stand opposite each other on the stage, unrolling between them as they went a large cloth on which dark clouds had been painted. The cloth was attached to the two poles, making a fat roll on the right and a thin roll on the left. Terror walked up and down looking very important.

"We have here the beginning of the world," he said in a solemn voice. "In the beginning there was nothing. Just mist and cloud, dust and steam."

August the Clown stood on the left, and Death on the right. They turned the two poles so that the cloth rolled across from right to left. More clouds and mist rolled past, and the sun and the moon.

"Stop! Wait a minute!" called Terror and the cloth stopped moving. "We've forgotten the most important thing of all. We need actors, too. Who would like a part in my play?"

"How can we?" asked the rocking toy in his squeaky little voice. "We don't even know what it's about."

"If you join in you'll know soon enough," said Terror. "Because it's about life. Well, who's not afraid of having a go?"

The dolls and the animals said nothing. Some shuffled about anxiously on their little chairs, others pretended they hadn't heard.

"Ha, that's just what I thought," said Terror. "A bunch of lily-livered cowards. Afraid of what life has to offer!"

"I'll do it," said a deep voice. Teddy Bear stood up. With his hands in his pockets and a nonchalant expression, he jumped with one bound up on to the stage.

"Of course you will," said Terror. "The play's about what life has to offer. You come from a family of merchants and traders. You're bound to look at all offers. Anyone else?"

"This one'll come with you, too!"

Lanky Flop slid off the bed and pulled himself up on to the stage. "Is this where I should stand? Just tell me what you want me to do."

"You'll see soon enough. There's room for one more!"

It was deathly quiet in the room. The dolls waited anxiously to see which one of them would pluck up enough courage to take part in the fat tomcat's mysterious play. Then they heard a little voice call out: "I'll come with you!"

Sophie's legs were out of bed. "Lanky Flop, Lanky Flop, I want to go with you! And I do want to know what life has to offer!" she cried.

"Are you out of your mind?" said Terror. "You're not well. Back to bed with you, at once! We don't need little girls."

Sophie ran on to the stage. Quickly she took up a position next to Lanky Flop and said: "You said yourself that human beings appear in your play. I am a human being and I can talk, too. So there!"

The animals and the dolls were so delighted not to have to go up on to the stage themselves that they shouted happily: "Let her join in! The poor child has such a dull life otherwise!"

Terror lined the actors up, Teddy Bear in front. They had to hold on to one another.

"Start rolling!" called Terror. Death and August the Clown each began to turn their poles again and the cloth moved on a little.

At first Sophie could hear nothing but a soft whistling noise; she thought it must be in her own head. But the whistling grew louder and louder, as if a fierce wind was sweeping the earth. And then she heard the roaring of waves, towering waves in a seething ocean.

She wanted to clap her hands to her ears, but that would mean letting go of Lanky Flop. So she squeezed her eyes tight shut instead. After a little while she took a quick look at the cloth, which was now rolling past her at breakneck speed. And then she opened both her eyes wide.

Waves were smashing against rocks and weird sea monsters were crawling up out of the foaming water. Overhead, in a threatening sky, dragon-headed birds the size of aeroplanes flapped past. Deserts went by, and trees and ferns pushed up through the earth's crust.

Sophie felt the ground under her feet tilt and shake; she was going to have to run whether she wanted to or not. She held on tight to Lanky Flop's shoulders and felt like screaming out loud, but no sound would come from her parched throat. She wanted to be sick and her head was heavy and hot as if it were full of burning rocks.

"My temperature must be up again," she thought. "And where's my room gone? And my dolls and my animals? But Lanky Flop's here, thank goodness. Oh, yes, we were going to act in a play . . ."

It was quiet. It was so quiet that Sophie could hear the soft patter of the raindrops falling on the trees. She was wet through. And her feet wouldn't stop moving. Tired and cold, she kept on dragging herself along the wet, sandy cart-track. A few yards in front of her she could see Terror and Lanky Flop bent double as they struggled against the lashing gusts of rain.

The Family

Through her wet eyelashes, Sophie could see an oatfield. The brown stalks bowed down to the earth, heavy with water. Sophie's feet hurt. For months she had lain between soft sheets and now she had been running through wet, loose sand for she couldn't tell how long. The tender skin on her feet had gone red and started to bleed. But she didn't notice because there was so much to see and to smell all around her.

In the oak coppice, raindrops bounced on the leaves. Smells of all kinds rose up, smells of moss and wood, grass, wet sand and birds' nests, mushrooms and snails. Sophie could not tell these smells apart. If you are kept indoors all the time and are not even allowed to stand at the open window, you forget the way things smell.

"Look out!" shouted Lanky Flop and pulled Sophie on to the grass verge.

A carriage drawn by two fiery horses was racing towards them at full tilt, rattling and clattering across the deep ruts.

The poor wretches, there by the side of

the road! They happened to be standing right next to a deep puddle. In a trice the carriage had passed them and they were left even wetter than before, spattered now with mud from head to toe.

"Did you see?" cried Sophie. "That was Teddy Bear in there!"

"Oh, yes, he'll be sitting pretty in the warm and dry, all right, you can be sure of that. Teddy Bear isn't one for walking about in the rain," said Terror. He spat and arched his back.

"Did you plan it like that?" asked Sophie.

"Plan it, what do you mean . . .? Ah, you don't understand anything, do you!"

"Come on, let's get going," said Lanky Flop, and held out his hand to Sophie.

She had to take two steps to each of his. Terror plodded along behind. And it never stopped raining.

A little way off to one side of the road, in a field, stood a tumbledown hut. Lanky Flop

made straight for it, through the long wet grass.

"Are we going to shelter from the rain?" asked Sophie.

"We'll see," said Lanky Flop.

He knocked on the door and pushed it open a crack. Inside it was dark. A shrill voice shrieked: "What do you want? Go away! Go away!"

A woman, all skin and bones, came to the door. To begin with, Sophie was sure she must be a witch. But she wasn't.

"There's nothing here for beggars!" screeched the woman. "We have nothing for ourselves, let alone for anyone else."

Lanky Flop leant against the doorpost, chewing on a straw and scratching his head. Then he gave a sheepish laugh. "That's a fine welcome," he said.

"Go peddle your jokes somewhere else," said the woman. "Hey, wait a minute, hey, is that you, Lanky Flop?"

"Oh, yes, indeedy, Lanky is my name," chuckled Lanky Flop.

"Well, you'd better come inside then," said the woman, but it didn't really sound as if she liked the idea much.

The three of them stepped into the dark hut. Lanky Flop had to duck. Then the woman suddenly burst into tears, threw her arms round Lanky Flop's neck and pressed her face to his chest.

A tiny fire was burning in the hearth. Five small children, dressed in rags, sat on the floor in front of it. And in a chair sat a man.

"Father, just look who's here! It's our Lanky!" said the woman.

"Have you got anything for us to eat, Mother?" asked Lanky Flop. "My stomach's rumbling like an empty coffin."

The man rose to his feet, kicked his chair over and came grim-faced to stand in front of Lanky Flop. Sophie crept anxiously behind Lanky Flop and peeped round his legs to watch what happened.

"Anything to eat?" said the man. His expression was fierce. "You mean to say you've come here empty-handed? When we haven't got anything to eat for ourselves? How dare you!"

"It's true," sobbed Lanky Flop's mother. "It's all because of the rain. It hasn't stopped raining for the past six weeks. There hasn't been so much as a single dry minute. The harvest is rotting in the fields. And the farmer doesn't care. No work, no money, he says. No money, no food."

Terror had found himself a corner by the hearth and was sitting licking himself clean all over. Sophie crept in beside him. But as soon as she could feel the warmth of that small fire, she began to shiver with the cold.

"I don't like it here much," Sophie whispered into Terror's ear. "Why didn't you plan it so that we could ride along with Teddy Bear in that nice carriage? If you planned this as well then I don't think much of it."

At first Terror pretended that he hadn't heard her. He kept his eyes shut tight and twitched his whiskers. But a moment later he started to wash his front paw and whispered: "Planning doesn't exist, get that into your head. You wanted to know everything – don't worry, you will. Now, since this is the first day, I'll let it go at that, but please don't talk about it any more. Or else I'll have to send you back to August the Clown and to Death, understand?"

Sophie had to set her mind working hard over this. She had a glimmering of an idea what "Death" was. But August the Clown? Who was that again? It was most peculiar: she couldn't remember anything from before that walk in the countryside through the rain.

Lanky Flop's father went out of the door, slamming it loudly behind him.

"He's off to inspect his traps," said Lanky Flop's mother. "If he wasn't such a good poacher we'd all have starved to death by now."

Darkness fell outside. The little children sat sobbing quietly in a corner. All they had had to eat that evening was a crust of mouldy bread and a cup of watery soup.

After supper old rags and tatters were spread out on the floor. The whole family lay down to sleep. Sophie, too, lay down, in among all the skinny unwashed children, Lanky Flop's little brothers and sisters. Soon afterwards the sound of gentle snoring was heard in the hut.

Sophie couldn't sleep. Carefully, afraid of waking the others, she sat up. Her eyes were used to the dark. She could see Lanky Flop sitting in his father's chair. He was awake too. His father hadn't come back home yet. Terror lay so close to the glowing ashes in the fireplace that his fur had nearly singed. He blinked his eyes, little green lights that seemed to flash on and off.

Lanky Flop stood up and stretched himself. "You two stay here," he said, so softly that they could hardly hear him. "I'll be back before morning."

"Can't I go with you?" Sophie whispered.

"No," said Lanky Flop, "nothing doing. I can't use a girl for what I'm going to do."

"Then promise you'll be back soon. Don't leave me alone here," pleaded Sophie.

Lanky Flop walked out of the door without replying. Terror lay asleep, or pretending that he was, his lips curled in a disdainful sneer.

It was the dead of night. Outside it was pitch dark. A heavy band of clouds chased across

the sky; now and then a few stars peeped through.

With his long legs Lanky Flop kept up a brisk pace. He leapt across a ditch, ran straight across a field of rye, climbed over a hedge and found himself in the farmer's kitchen garden. Suddenly he bumped into someone.

"Hello, good evening," said Lanky Flop. "And who might you be?"

No answer.

"What an uncivil fellow you are! I said: Good evening!" Lanky Flop put out his hands. He felt a coat and two arms that seemed to be about to embrace him. "You must have fallen on your face and lost your tongue," chuckled Lanky Flop. "It's not good enough, see!" And he slapped the man on his shoulder. The man swayed from side to side but still said nothing at all.

Just at the moment the moon came out, and Lanky Flop could see who was standing in front of him: it was the Scarecrow. Lanky Flop gave him a deep bow and said: "Oh, so it's you! You don't mind if I borrow your clothes, do you? I'll bring them straight back."

He put the Scarecrow's hat on his head and stuffed some straw under it, then pulled on his coat. Stiff-legged he walked on.

The watchdog outside the farmhouse began to bark. He flew out of his kennel and went for Lanky Flop, as far as his chain would let him.

"Shhh! Don't make such a row. Can't you see who I am?" said Lanky Flop.

"Oh, it's you," said the watchdog. "What do you want? I've never seen you up here before."

"I just wanted to have a look to see what it's like," said Lanky Flop. "You think it's fun standing still all the time? It's great, stretching your legs." He walked stiffly round the dog, as if his legs were made out of two sticks. "Tell me, do you know where the sparrows and starlings are nesting?"

"The sparrows are in the trees and the starlings are under the thatched roof," said the dog.

"That's what I thought," said Lanky Flop. "Now, if you make sure to keep absolutely quiet, then you'll be a really good watchdog. Because I want to teach those birds a lesson, see? They may be all tucked away nicely in their nests right now, but as soon as the sun comes out, they'll be back eating up all the seeds in my garden again. Get it?"

The dog understood. Quietly he lay there, watching as Lanky Flop shinned the drainpipe to the roof of the farmhouse.

Lanky Flop let himself down through the wide chimney, and finished up in a large kitchen.

"This farmer certainly isn't going hungry," he said softly, looking round at the rows of hams and sausages hanging from the beams. The bread-bin was crammed with freshly baked loaves; cheeses were spread out along a shelf. And in the pantry he found racks of eggs, pots of jam, a barrel of butter, a roast partridge and a collection of sweetmeats, fruits and pastries, the like of which he had never seen before.

Lanky Flop began to fill his pockets. He shoved the eggs under his hat, two hams disappeared down his trousers, a side of bacon and a large flat cheese went under his coat.

"I'll need a bag for the bread," he said, "but first I'll have a good look round." He tiptoed through the house.

In the parlour, his eyes widened. What beautiful things the farmer had! But there was nothing there that Lanky Flop needed. Except for a couple of cigars, which he stuck

behind his ears. "One for Father and one for me. Fair's fair," he said with a grin.

Upstairs was the bedroom, which reverberated with loud snoring. Lanky Flop went from one bed to the other. First he looked at the farmer and his wife, who were both enormously fat. In the other bed lay two fat girls, while the farmhand slept in the built-in closet-bed. They had all eaten far too much; they wouldn't have woken up if a cannon had been fired in the room. But they could snore, all right, and there were hearty rumblings under the bedclothes from all the food inside their stomachs.

On the bedside table next to the farmer lay a golden watch. Lanky Flop held it to his ear and listened to the ticking. Nodding thoughtfully, he put the watch down again. Then he blew out the candle and went back down to the kitchen. He filled a sack with bread and climbed out through the chimney.

The dog wagged his tail. "Any luck?" he asked. "Did you teach those birds a lesson?"

"They wouldn't wake up," said Lanky Flop. "Talk about sleep, you've never seen anything like it. But I took their eggs away with me, just look." And he lifted his hat.

The dog looked at him suspiciously and growled. "You look funny to me," he said. "If you ask me, you've grown fatter on top. Hey! What's that? What's that you've got under your coat?"

"You know, if everyone did his duty like you, the world would be a much better

place," said Lanky Flop. "It's the likes of us, you and me, who make sure that the thieves don't get away with it. If they did, even the rich would have to go out into the streets and beg."

"How right you are," said the dog, and wagged his tail.

"And if there were no more rich people and the countryside was full of nothing but beggars, who would be there to give those poor wretches a crust of bread?" said Lanky Flop.

"Good thinking," said the dog. "It's nice to have a chat once in a while with someone who's got a good head on his shoulders. Now at least I know that there is another honest soul on this farm. When they let me off the chain in the morning, I'll come and look you up. But you'd best get back to your place now – the sun's about to come up."

Lanky Flop went off to the kitchen garden, stowed all the food in a few empty potato sacks and put the clothes back on the Scarecrow.

And in the grey light of dawn he hastened back to his mother's and father's little house.

They ate and drank until they could eat and drink no more. Then they would doze off

for a while, but as soon as they woke they would begin to eat and to drink all over again.

Lanky Flop's little brothers and sisters climbed up on to his lap and his shoulders and pulled at his hair. They laughed at everything and at nothing.

By evening, everybody was queasy. Each in turn would disappear outside and be sick. The stench by the door was horrible.

Sophie was the only one not to be sick. She hadn't eaten nearly as much as the rest, for she had a small stomach. That was probably because she had been ill for so long, or perhaps because all her life she had only eaten dainty little helpings beautifully prepared just for her.

"Well, so long, then," said Lanky Flop next day. "I think I've done my bit. My compliments and all the best to you all!"

And he walked out of the door. Sophie and Terror followed him out. All the little brothers and sisters came running after them, keeping up with them until they reached the farmer's field. Lanky Flop looked back and saw that his mother had already shut the door of the little house. "She thinks she's on to a good thing," he said, "but that's not what I had in mind." And he shouted at the children: "Off you go, off, off, off, back to the house with you! Who's going to be the first to get there?"

"No, no!" said the children. "We want to stay with you."

"Not a chance," said Lanky Flop. "Off you go or I'll smack you."

"And what about her?" called one of the brothers and pointed at Sophie.

"She's quite a different matter," said Lanky Flop. He put his arm round Sophie and called: "On your way, or it'll be the worse for you!"

Terror went and stood in the middle of the road. He arched his back, made all his hair stand up on end, and began to spit. The children fell quiet and stood looking anxiously at the angry tomcat. Lanky Flop picked up a stone and made as if to throw it at them. Sophie couldn't help laughing.

"Hurry up now! Run! Run!" Lanky Flop shouted, and began chasing the children down the road.

And, cross and scared, back home they went.

The Bog

Towards evening they met up with a group of travellers searching the countryside for food and work. The travellers had a cart drawn by a bag-of-bones of a horse and crammed with all their goods and chattels. A sick old woman lay in the cart on top of everything. All the others walked, men, women and children.

Lanky Flop, Sophie and Terror joined them.

The children would be sent off to beg from the farms and the women would try to sell needles and brushes. Whenever they passed through a village, the men would make music and a few of the girls would perform a dance. They had a puppet theatre, too, with a dog, Toby, who collected the money.

Sophie would sometimes help the puppeteer. She quickly learned all his acts by heart, and would pass him the puppets whenever he gave a performance. His wife hardly ever felt like giving him a hand.

And so a few weeks passed. By day they would travel, perform in the villages and collect money. As soon as it grew dark, they would light a fire and lie down to sleep in the woods. Often there wasn't enough food to go round and then there would be quarrels and fights. Sometimes it rained and sometimes the sun shone. But it didn't matter which, every day seemed much like the next.

The puppeteer's wife had fiery eyes and long, wild, wavy hair. All the men and boys in the group tried to walk next to her.

Her name was Annabella.

Sophie thought Annabella was beautiful, but she was also frightened of her. One moment Annabella would be happy, laughing and cracking jokes, and letting the boys give her a squeeze. And the next, she would be angry or sulky, fretting and crying. And you never knew which it was going to be.

One day Sophie woke up before dawn. In the east, the sky was just turning grey. Terror lay asleep next to her. Lanky Flop was nowhere to be seen.

On hands and knees, Sophie crawled carefully through all the people, searching for Lanky Flop. A little distance away from the rest, by a tree, she could hear whispering. Two people were lying there, frolicking about under a blanket.

"Hey, you handsome spellbinder, I wouldn't mind giving it a go with you. I've been fed up with that old goat of a puppeteer for a long time. What do you say? Will you be sure to see I get enough to eat?"

"I'll take care of everything, keep your hair on!"

It was Lanky Flop and Annabella!

"Just the two of us," whispered Annabella. "We don't need any of the others. But you will make sure there's plenty of food, won't you, sweetheart? It may be fashionable to look skinny, but no one wants a washboard. Right?"

Sophie saw Lanky Flop sit up and chuckle.

"Come on then, quick!" said Annabella. She got to her feet and pulled Lanky Flop up. Together they went off into the wood.

In no time at all there was nothing more to be seen of them. Sophie wanted to call out but she couldn't make a sound. She wanted to cry, but couldn't manage that either. And so she just stood there, shivering in the chilly dawn, until she heard a gentle grumbling noise behind her and felt something soft brush along her arm.

"Shhh, don't be frightened. We'll follow them," whispered Terror.

There were lots of broken branches lying about between the trees. Terror could climb over them without making a noise but Sophie couldn't. Now and then they would both jump when she put her foot on a branch and it snapped with a loud crack. When they reached the edge of the wood, they saw a big bog stretching away into the distance.

"That stupid fool," muttered Terror. "Whatever possessed him to make off with that female? He should have asked me first, as well he knows."

Sophie peered out into the half-light. "Where have they gone?" she asked.

"Over there, there's a path across the bog. I can see them all right."

"Why should he have asked you first?" whispered Sophie.

"Goodness gracious, have you forgotten everything already? Have you?"

Forgotten? What had she forgotten? A wrinkle appeared at the top of her nose from the hard thinking she was doing. Vaguely she could see a few things, a cupboard, a chimney, a row of small chairs with dolls sitting on them. What did it all mean? Had she ever come across any of them? And if so, where?

Squalls of fine raindrops swept across the countryside. Slowly it grew lighter and Sophie could see two shadowy figures that appeared to be walking across the bog. She couldn't be expected to think when everything was in such a muddle! She brushed the wet hair out of her eyes and said: "We've got to catch up with them."

The path across the bog was narrow but firm under foot. Quickly they set out along it.

"What are they going to do? Do you know?" asked Sophie.

"I'd rather not tell you," said Terror. "Whatever happens, happens, and you mustn't worry your head about it. Hang on! Did you hear that?"

They stopped.

"Help! Help!"

It was coming from the bog, somewhere in the distance to the side of the path. Sophie could see that Lanky Flop and Annabella had stopped too. A flock of crows, cawing loudly, flew overhead. A sudden gust of wind blew the rain hard into their faces.

"Help me! Please help me! I'm sinking!" they heard someone cry.

"Wait a minute, who is that? Haven't we met before?" shouted Lanky Flop. "If I'm not mistaken, that's Teddy Bear!"

"Teddy Bear!" called Sophie. "It's Teddy Bear, my Teddy Bear!" And she started to run. When she caught up with Lanky Flop she clung to him. "Thank goodness you're here," she gasped.

"Lanky Flop!" called Teddy Bear from the bog. "Heaven be praised! God Himself has sent me a strong, stout-hearted lad to get me out of here. As soon as I get back to town, I'll show my gratitude. I'll have Masses said, at least fifty of them, and I'll give a playroom to the orphanage, and a peal of bells to the church . . . and . . . you only have to say . . . Oh, Lanky Flop, my best, my very dearest friend! Save me! Quickly! I'm sinking deeper and deeper!"

"Is that how you'd spend your money to show your gratitude?" called Lanky Flop. "Saying Masses and all that kind of rubbish? Can't you think of anything better? If I were in your shoes, I certainly would. Hey, come on, say something! I can only just see you. How deep have you sunk in now?"

"Oh, help him, please, save him, quickly!" Sophie pleaded.

"As far as where the ends of my legs come," called Teddy Bear.

"That could mean either your feet or your backside," said Lanky Flop. "But I think I get the picture: you're up to your unmentionables in it. Do you know why that's happened, hey, Teddy Bear? Your coat pockets are too full, that's why. You've got too much money in them, my boy, much too much money. That's heavy stuff, that is, it's bound to drag you down."

"What shall I do? Help me! Help me!"

"Listen! Tie all your money in your handkerchief and throw it over here. You'll see how light you are then. No kidding, you'll be safe and sound all right when you've done that."

For some time they could hear nothing from the bog but groans and soft sobs. Then something came flying towards them and landed with a soft plop on the path.

Annabella burst into peals of laughter. She slapped her bottom and her thighs, she bent over double, then threw her head back again with glee. Quickly she snatched up the handkerchief filled with money and tucked it away down her cleavage inside the top of

her dress. "Come on!" she cried and grabbed Lanky Flop's hand.

"Kind regards!" called Lanky Flop. "And all the very best!"

Rooted to the spot, her eyes wide with shock, Sophie watched Lanky Flop allowing

himself to be dragged off by Annabella. Nudging her, Terror said softly: "Well, you did want to know what life had to offer, didn't you?"

"Yes, I did," said Sophie without stopping to think or paying attention. "And also what happens after you're dead. But that was a mean thing to do!" And she ran after Lanky Flop, tugged at his arm and cried: "We've got to save him! Now! There's no time to lose!"

Lanky Flop looked long and hard at her, then gave a nod and said: "All right, let's get going then."

It was as if a great coloured soap bubble had taken off deep inside Sophie. First she flung her arms round Lanky Flop's neck and kissed him on both cheeks, then she ran back to Terror, who had stayed close to the spot where Teddy Bear was stuck in the bog, and began hopping from one foot to the other.

"Keep calm," Terror said. "Everyone take off your clothes."

Annabella refused to join in. Arms akimbo, her face contorted with rage, she stood and watched while Sophie and Lanky Flop took off their clothes and spread them out over the swampy ground.

Terror lay down flat on his stomach and began creeping backwards towards Teddy Bear. Sophie followed him, holding on tight to Terror's front paws. Then Lanky Flop, too, stretched his long body out along the soggy ground and held on to Sophie's legs. Teddy Bear grabbed hold of Terror's tail and the whole line tried slowly, very, very slowly, to crawl back to the edge.

At first it looked as if Teddy Bear was stuck too tightly in the mud. They pulled and pulled until Sophie felt just like a piece of elastic stretched as far as it would go. Then, hey presto: "PLOP!"; a jet of mud spurted up, and up came Teddy Bear with it. Flying over their heads in a graceful arc, he landed on the hard path, scrambled quickly to his feet, gave his filthy clothes a quick brush down and nodded graciously to Annabella.

"Oh, dearie me, let me do that for you," she said. "What a blessing you managed to get out of that."

She smiled at Teddy Bear, took a handkerchief out of her stocking top and began to clean him up. She even wiped the spatters of mud out of his eyes. Then she took him by the arm and walked off with him.

Cautiously Terror, Sophie and Lanky Flop crawled back to the path. There they picked up their dirty clothes and stood holding them up to the pouring rain. By the time they had rubbed themselves as clean as they could with tufts of grass, Teddy Bear and Annabella were nothing more than a couple of small specks in the distance.

In silence they followed them.

The Fair

They were wet, numb and tired. Their sodden clothes, heavy with sludge, clung to their bodies. Even Terror walked slowly, his fur caked with the squelchy mud.

Silently they moved forward. The rain was pouring down in torrents. Annabella and Teddy Bear were nowhere to be seen.

Finally they reached a town. Bustling crowds filled the streets; they were carried along in a stream of people. Lanky Flop walked in front. Sophie hung tightly to his arm, afraid of losing him. When they reached the market-place they realised why there were such crowds: it was the day of the annual fair.

"Ha, that smells good. Especially when you're dying of hunger," said Lanky Flop, making straight for a stall selling doughnuts. The greasy steam from the doughnuts made Sophie feel sick. And yet her mouth watered.

As soon as the fat red-faced woman turned her back to fish some freshly-made doughnuts out of the boiling oil, Lanky Flop snatched three doughnuts from the counter. He took off with them, running along behind the row of stalls with Terror and Sophie following close behind.

"Here," said Lanky Flop.

Sophie took a bite. It burned her tongue, tears sprang to her eyes and she said: "Stealing is wrong."

Then she took another bite.

"If you're hungry, you've got to steal," said Lanky Flop.

"Terror, it's true, isn't it?" said Sophie. "Stealing is wrong."

"All right then, if that's how you feel, I'll go off and get some more but just for me

this time," said Lanky Flop. He told them to stay where they were and that he'd be back in a minute.

Terror finished his doughnut. He winked at Sophie and said: "Perhaps both of you are right."

They did not have long to wait for Lanky Flop. He came sauntering up with his hands behind his back and an innocent expression on his face.

"This is for you." He handed Sophie a pretzel and an apple. "And what do you say? Thank-you-very-much-dear-Lanky-Flop, that's what!"

He grinned and pulled a fried fish from under his hat for Terror. For himself he had taken half a roast cockerel.

"You'd have to be pretty stupid not to be able to fix yourself up with a few things at a fair like this," he said.

Terror licked his whiskers. "If you have any sense you don't steal. There's a very

good chance that you'll finish up behind bars," he said.

"All right, all right, fine words," said Lanky Flop. "Come on, let's take a look round."

There was a lot to see at the fair. Not only were there all sorts of things for sale, there was a puppet show as well and a rope dancer doing his act high above the crowd. And they watched a man keeping eight balls in the air at the same time by catching and tossing them up over and over again.

In a corner there were some low carts with cages on them. Amazing creatures were locked up inside so that people could look at them.

In the cages there was the fattest lady in the world and a calf with two heads and five legs. A man sitting on a chair had a kind of trunk instead of a nose. And his face was covered all over with short white hair. When his eyes met Sophie's, she could see that he had the eyes of an ordinary person, except that they were terribly sad. But she thought the calf was the saddest of all since it was scarcely able to lift its two heavy heads, and had to let them hang pitifully down to the ground.

The owner of these extraordinary creatures waved his collecting box under their noses. Lanky Flop quickly dragged them into the crowd in case there was an argument or even a fight.

"Hey, what's that?" said Sophie and walked up to a raised platform on which stood a pair of huge copper scales. One was inscribed PROGRESS AND HAPPINESS, the other one said MISERY.

A strangely attired man with a label reading "Director" on his hat was grinding away at a small barrel organ. It played a happy little tune. More and more people crowded up to have a look at the remarkable

scales, and quite soon the director stopped playing.

"Ladies and gentlemen!" he shouted. "Roll up! Roll up! Come and discover the truth about mankind's fate! Come and learn what life has to offer! Roll up! Roll up!"

A small boy walked round rattling a tin. He started at the back of the crowd, so Lanky Flop, Terror and Sophie had time to stay and watch.

"Behold the scales of life," exclaimed the director. "These scales are at all times in balance. Whosoever takes or whosoever is given anything from one of these scales must also take or be given something from the other. That's how it has been for century upon century, year after year, day in, day out.

"Pay careful attention now, good people. And don't imagine you have any say in the matter. Because you do not. Oh, no! Watch closely now, first we extract some misery from this scale here, the one on your left . . ."

He brought out a placard attached to a long pole and held it up. It pictured a gruesome scene: a house in flames, people stabbing each other to death with knives, and a child hollow-eyed with hunger.

"Behold, a fine helping of misery and sorrow, yes, indeed, yes, indeed," said the

director. "That's going to put our scales badly out of balance. But look here . . ." and, hey presto, he had thrust another picture high in the air. They saw a beautiful landscape, ripe wheat stacked in sheaves in the fields, a half-built cathedral with workmen carrying bricks and planks about, and in the foreground a man with a table napkin round his neck making the most of a sumptuous meal.

"Progress and happiness!" said the director. "Does misery strike in one part of the world? Then at the very same moment there will be people enjoying health, wealth and prosperity in another. That's how our spinning globe is always kept in balance. If it weren't so, then the earth would go hurtling out of orbit and vanish behind the sun!

"Which one of you will come up here and help me give a demonstration of these magnificent, forever balanced, scales of life?"

"I will!" cried Sophie. She clambered up on the platform without noticing Terror's attempts to hold her back.

"Just look at this brave young lady, everybody," said the director. The audience began to laugh and shout. "Tell us, girl, from which of the scales would you like to be served?"

"From this one," said Sophie, and pointed to the scale with PROGRESS AND HAPPINESS written on it. The people yelled and laughed even more loudly.

"And what is it to be? Just say what you would like to have."

Sophie looked round her shyly. Then she saw Lanky Flop standing there in his filthy rags, shoulders hunched, looking cross and impatient.

"I know!" she said. "A nice warm coat for Lanky Flop!"

Even before she had finished speaking a lovely coat with a fur collar floated up out of the copper scale with PROGRESS AND HAPPINESS on it.

"Here, that's for you," said Sophie, and held out the coat to Lanky Flop.

She turned to jump happily off the platform, but the director seized her by the arm and pulled her back.

"Ho, ho!" he said. "That's what you think! Whosoever takes from one scale shall also be given from the other. But you'll be able to give that away too, with a good conscience. Well, what is it to be?" He pointed to the scale on the right.

To her horror, Sophie could see that the scales had begun to move. They were clumping slowly along the wooden platform as if about to stump right up to where she stood. The scale called MISERY hung lower than the other, and Sophie was afraid that something horrible would spill over the rim at any moment: red-hot lava, or fiery tongues that would slither down the side and blow the burning breath of sickness and decay into people's faces.

"I don't know," she stammered. "You say. Something just for myself, please."

"No one gets anything for nothing in this life," said the director, "and a warm coat with a fur collar is no small thing. So you choose. The loss of both eyes? A crippled leg? Which do you want?"

"No, no!" cried Sophie.

The throbbing and hissing in the MISERY scale grew louder and louder, everyone held his breath, and the director bawled at her: "Get a move on! If you're not going to choose then I'll have to do it for you!"

Sophie clapped her hands to her eyes. Suddenly she felt an icy blast on her head and her hair stood straight up on end. She

tried to hold on to it, but she could feel it being sucked away between her fingers. And she was powerless to stop it.

"Ooooh!" came from the crowd in the market-place.

There it went, Sophie's lovely long hair. It floated away through the air and in a moment had disappeared over the rooftops. The scales had stopped moving. The director took up his barrel organ and began to grind it again.

Sophie's head was a pale smooth ball, like the full moon in winter. Quickly Terror and Lanky Flop dragged her away. The crowd pressed round them, jeering at the ridiculous sight of the little girl with her bald head. And it was all her own fault.

They crossed the market-place, Lanky Flop in the new coat that fitted him as if it had been made to measure, Terror walking quietly but quickly, and Sophie with her hands covering her head and a face scarlet with mortification.

The merry notes of the barrel organ sounded farther and farther away.

A Home and a Prison

Aimlessly they ran through a maze of streets and narrow alleyways, paying little attention to where they were going. They had no idea, after all, of their way round the town, or where they would be spending the night.

"Stop!" called Terror, and came to a halt outside a doorway with a barred gate. "We're rushing about as if we're going to be late for something. Just where are we rushing to, anyway?"

"Are you tired?" Lanky Flop asked in a surprised tone of voice.

"No, I'm not tired, I just want to have a think. What are we going to do? You two tell me!"

"I'm tired even if you're not," said Sophie. She leaned against the gate, and a bell began to jangle. Sophie didn't notice; she was admiring Lanky Flop's distinguished appearance in his beautiful new coat.

"Now look what you've done!" exclaimed Lanky Flop. "I don't know what's the matter with you, you just do one stupid thing after another."

Sophie quickly stood up straight and the jangling stopped. But it was too late: a woman was coming down the garden path at a trot towards them. She had felt slippers on and her long white skirt fluttered about her legs.

The woman stuck her pointed nose between the bars of the gate and looked at Sophie. Then she began to laugh, and her laughter completely changed her face, which became gentle and friendly. She opened the gate.

"Come in quickly, my little one," she said.

Sophie blushed. "It was a mistake, ma'am," she stammered. "I didn't mean to ring, it happened by accident."

"That doesn't matter," said the woman. "Come in, but be quick."

Lanky Flop pushed Sophie to one side. "She's a bit confused today," he said. "Honestly, we were just passing and then she leaned against the bell. Sorry to have troubled you."

"That's what they usually say," said the woman. She walked through the gate, took Sophie's hand and led her a little way up the street. Then she turned round, pointed at the doorway and said: "There you are, can you see it now?"

Above the doorway some letters had been carved in the stone. They read HOME FOR UNFORTUNATE CHILDREN. The woman put her arm round Sophie and before Sophie knew what was happening she was standing in the garden. Behind her the gate's lock clicked shut.

"Visiting hours Sundays from two to four. Family only," the woman said to Terror and Lanky Flop.

The garden was beautiful. Rose trees on slender stems stood in circular flower-beds, red roses, pink roses and roses of a wonderfully soft whitish, or creamy, colour. Round

HOME FOR
UNFORTUNATE CHILDREN

the flower-beds there were borders of forget-me-nots and pansies. Sophie never even looked back once.

They came to a large house, walked round the outside and went in through the back door.

"Run upstairs now," said the woman, "to the playroom. You'll have no trouble finding it."

Sophie went slowly up the broad staircase. At the top she came to a passage with a great many doors and could tell at once where the playroom was, although she didn't dare go in. There were a lot of sounds behind one of the doors: talking, laughing and singing. And the noise of building blocks dropping on the floor, balls bouncing against the wall, the clicking of knitting needles, the tumbling of ninepins, the rustling of tissue paper, the racing of nimble feet on a wooden floor and the soft thumping of children doing somersaults on a mat.

Sophie peered through the keyhole: she could see nothing at all. But just as she stood there, bending down with her eye to the keyhole, the door flew open and she fell into the room.

Hurriedly she scrambled to her feet, wishing she could make herself tiny and invisible since there were at least thirty children in the large room, all of whom had stopped playing and were looking at her. Sophie hugged the wall and looked at the floor.

Almost at once the same sounds that she had heard in the passage began again. The children had gone back to their play.

Cautiously she peeped through her eyelashes. Then she forgot to be afraid or shy. All the children were busy with some game or other, by themselves or in groups of three or four. No one paid any attention to her, there was no screaming and no squabbling.

Sophie could still remember vividly what things had been like when she had gone to school, before she had fallen ill. She remembered all the shoving, the kicking and the pinching, the name-calling and snatching and teasing and tale-telling of the children in her class. She had never much liked being with a lot of children.

But these children were different. They didn't come up to her with prying faces, pestering her with questions. They didn't start jeering when they saw her standing there with her head as bald as the moon on a winter's night. They had all stopped looking at her.

Then a boy came up to her. He only had one leg and limped along with a crutch under his arm. He smiled at her. He didn't laugh at her. He just smiled at her.

"Want to join in?" the boy asked. "We're building a castle."

Those were wonderful days Sophie spent in the Home for Unfortunate Children. The woman who had let her in was called Auntie by everyone. She looked after all the children but fortunately the looking-after wasn't very obvious. The children were busy all day long without anyone telling them what they had to do.

They helped in the kitchen and outside in the grounds. Behind the house there was an overgrown garden, and beyond that was the kitchen garden. Those who wanted to

worked. There was always plenty to do. The children also made their own beds and mopped the floors. Everyone did what they could, as a matter of course. Now and then Auntie would ask them for something; she

never gave orders. When there was no work to do the children would play. They taught one another to read and to write. The bigger ones read to the little ones and helped them with their sewing and knitting.

Auntie understood children. She knew that children are not lazy by nature, that they like being busy all day long and love doing useful things.

Sophie joined in everything. At night she felt pleasantly tired and fell asleep as soon as she climbed between the sheets. She had never before been so content.

It only took a couple of days for her to find out exactly what was the matter with each of the children. They all had something that used to worry them before they came to the Home. One of them had a stammer; another wore thick glasses; there was a girl who had almost no nose and a boy with water on the brain. The boy with one leg was always smiling; he seemed to have a face that smiled no matter what happened.

And there were children who looked as if there was nothing much the matter with

them. But there was something wrong with them too. One couldn't learn to read and another was terribly frightened of water. A third couldn't speak. Even the cat was a little bit unfortunate: it was frightened of mice.

Every morning Sophie would examine herself anxiously in the mirror. Had any more hair grown back on her head? As soon as her hair had grown back properly she would have to leave, for she would no longer be an unfortunate child then. And she very much wanted to stay. Perhaps she ought to tell Auntie about her illness. And that she didn't have much longer to live. Or wouldn't that count?

And so the days passed until it was Sunday. And then everything changed.

By one o'clock Sophie was standing by the gate waiting. "Who knows, they could be early," she told herself.

Under her arm she had a small doll, one of the Home's toys. It had become her favourite and she always had it with her. The little doll even slept in her bed. That wasn't really allowed but Sophie pushed it right down under the bedclothes as far as her feet so that no one could tell.

A few parents had arrived and stood about waiting on the other side of the gate for visiting time to start. After a while there were lots of people, men and women, young and old. They had unhappy faces and pretended they couldn't see Sophie.

"Well, it can't be much fun having an unfortunate child," Sophie thought and put her hand up to her bald head. Some stiff little points were already coming through, like the prickles on a rosehip. You couldn't see them yet, only feel them.

There was no sign of Lanky Flop and Terror. Wherever had they got to? By the time the gate had opened at two o'clock and all the parents had crowded in, there was still no sign of them. Sophie had been pushed to one side, and then suddenly she saw Terror, hidden behind the wall. He grabbed hold of her and pulled her out into the street. The gate fell shut.

"Quick, come on!" he said, and made off at a trot, turned a corner and stopped.

"Where is Lanky Flop?" asked Sophie.

"I'll come to that in a minute," said Terror. "Something has happened. You can't stay on in the Home now. I had to take you out like that because I didn't know whether they'd let you go. It's a good thing you were standing so close to the gate. I say, what's that you've got under your arm?"

"What has happened? And where is Lanky Flop?"

"Well, it's a long story. All in good time. But what have you got there?" Terror pointed to the little doll. Sophie pressed it tightly to her chest with both her hands.

"This is Ulliput," she said.

"Ulliput," said Terror scornfully. "A doll!

Throw it away right now, do you hear, you can't drag that thing around with you. It'll make things much too difficult."

"No!" said Sophie. She turned round and stuffed Ulliput inside her nightdress, so that only a little bit of her bonnet could be seen.

"Lanky Flop is in prison," said Terror.

"Oooooh!" Sophie said, clapping her hands to her face with shock.

They walked on slowly until they came to a park. Then they sat down on a bench.

"Yes, my child, I'm afraid that's what's happened. There he is on nothing but bread and water, that fine friend of yours," Terror began. "And that coat you gave him, he's managed to get rid of that already too. Swapped it for a few guilders, I believe.

"Anyway, what happened was this: we found work. In a warehouse. Lanky Flop as a dock-hand and I, because I have the brains for it, in the office. Counting goods all day long and writing everything down. Tedious and boring . . ."

"And Lanky Flop?" asked Sophie.

"The work was hard, that I must say. Heaving sacks of rags and tatters about. Up

ladder, down ladder, then outside across a gangplank to one of the boats at the quayside. He didn't much care for it, as you can imagine. He's not cut out for work, your Lanky Flop."

"Oh, no?" said Sophie. "He can climb, he can run really fast, he can . . . he can creep about so softly that you can't hear him . . . Lanky Flop is terribly clever!"

"Exactly. He's very good at doing all those things. But working for twelve hours on end, working hard, mind you, so that he pleases his boss, that he can't do.

"The first day, it was still all right. He really did his best. After that there was nothing but trouble. He would sneak off and take a nap in some corner so that the other dock-hands had to do his work for him. You should have heard the foreman curse! And the boss would come round quite often too, because it didn't take him long to get wise to Lanky Flop. He would spin his gold watch on his gold watch chain – then you had to watch out! He only did it because he was nervous, of course.

"And meanwhile I was sitting in the office counting and calculating. Sometimes I managed to dash off a short poem on the back of an envelope. Never more than three or four lines, though."

"Yes, but what about Lanky Flop?" Sophie asked impatiently.

"Well, as far as he was concerned the work was too hard and the wages too low. Mind you, he wasn't all that wrong either. We'd rented a small room and there wasn't enough left over for food.

"It happened yesterday. The boss was standing there again, twirling his watch on account of his nerves. Suddenly Lanky Flop leapt at him and snatched the watch out of his hand, chain and all. Very agile, I have to admit. Then he took to his heels, Lanky Flop did. And can he run! They all ran after him, the dock-hands, the foreman and the boss. Me too, of course, because I had to know what happened.

"At first it looked as if he was going to shake them all off. But then the police turned up. Three officers. They nabbed him just as he was about to sell the watch to a junk dealer for a hundred guilders. What a fool!"

Sophie sat staring in front of her saying

nothing. She had taken Ulliput out of her nightdress and was cradling her in her arms. Terror went on: "Now he's in the clink. With a chain on his leg and a heavy iron ball on the end. He gets nothing to eat but a bit of bread and water and at night there are rats. They keep him awake gnawing at his toes."

Sophie was crying. She cried without making any noise. The tears streamed in such a flood from her sorrowful eyes that her nightdress and Ulliput the doll were soaked through. The tears poured and poured until there was a puddle on the floor. Some sparrows came to take a bath in it.

"May I see him?" she asked. "Do they have visiting hours there too?"

"We'll try," said Terror. "If you've quite finished crying we'll go and see."

A guard was sitting in front of the prison door. He had leant his gun up against the wall. When Terror and Sophie came closer they could see that he was fast asleep.

The door was secured with three heavy padlocks. At the top there was a little shuttered grille.

"Stand on my back, then you'll be able to see inside," said Terror.

Sophie climbed on to Terror's back. It was dark in the cell and at first she could see nothing at all. "Lanky Flop, are you there?" she called.

She heard a chain being dragged across the stone floor. Lanky Flop's face appeared on the other side of the little grille. Sophie gave a very deep sigh.

"Oh, Lanky Flop! My dear, dear Lanky Flop!" she said in a whisper.

"Is that you, little Sophie?" said Lanky Flop. "Have you been crying? You mustn't do that, my little baldyhead – girls get ugly that way."

"Oh, Lanky Flop!" said Sophie again. "I wish you weren't in prison!"

Lanky Flop looked ill, pale and tired. He smiled and said: "It can't be helped. Life's like that. Sometimes you're lucky and sometimes you're not. After all, you wanted to know what life has to offer, didn't you? Now, little Sophie, listen carefully. You must get away from here. With Terror. Run away with him as far as you can. You do what he tells you. I'm going to be hanged soon, so I'm no good to you any more."

Sophie couldn't utter another word. The tears were pouring down her cheeks.

"Hey, stop that!" urged Terror. "I don't

like getting wet."

The guard moved in his sleep and turned, still snoring, over on to his side.

"We'll get you out of there," whispered Sophie. "I promise! Shall I leave Ulliput with you in the meantime? Then you won't feel so lonely. I can easily slip her through the bars." She showed Ulliput to Lanky Flop.

"A doll?" said Lanky Flop. "You'd better hang on to her. I don't much care for dolls. Now let me have another word with Terror."

Sophie jumped off Terror's back. Lanky Flop and Terror whispered together for a long time. Occasionally they would look at Sophie, and then they would smile. For something had happened to Sophie. During the few minutes that she had been talking to Lanky Flop, the prickles on her head had grown. They had turned into beautiful soft little curls, like a layer of fluffy down.

The guard moved in his sleep again, turning right over this time. Quickly Sophie and Terror said goodbye to Lanky Flop. They went back to the little room Terror had rented.

That night neither of them could sleep a wink. For hours they sat up talking and making plans. They had to free Lanky Flop before he was hanged. There was one guard, Terror said, who might be willing to help. He would leave the door open when he brought Lanky Flop his jug of water and his mouldy bread. But they would have to give him five hundred guilders first.

"Buying him off, it's called," said Terror.

"Why not just call it buying?" Sophie said. "I don't understand the 'off' bit. You give the guard the money and you get Lanky Flop in exchange. Five hundred guilders is a lot of money, though, isn't it?"

"Yes, we'd never be able to save that much just having a job, that's for sure."

"Then we'll have to steal it."

"That's not a very good idea."

They sat there looking at each other gloomily. Not a sound was to be heard anywhere. Dark night lay over the town and everyone was asleep. Suddenly Sophie jumped up with a shout of cheerful laughter.

"Terror, Terror, I've got it!" she cried. "I know just what we'll do! We'll go and look for Teddy Bear, because he's rich. And he owes his life to Lanky Flop: Lanky Flop got him out of the bog. Teddy Bear will give us the money!"

She danced round Terror. At last they knew what to do. And since there was still an hour left to sleep, they crawled back into bed.

Bear House

They left early the next morning to look for Teddy Bear, asking all the people they met on the way how to get to his house. Teddy Bear must have been an important person since everyone they asked claimed to know him. First one sent them in this direction, then another sent them in that. And so they walked about all day long, to the north, to the east, to the south and to the west. But they didn't find Teddy Bear.

It was the first day of winter. Yellowish-grey clouds blanketed the sky and darkness fell early. Every now and then sleet fell. Towards the end of the afternoon it got so cold that Sophie became completely stiff and numb. Terror's tail dragged along the ground.

They were on the outskirts of the town, where the houses, elegant large villas set in beautiful gardens, were few and far between.

"Tomorrow is another day," said Terror. "We'll go as far as the next house and then we'll turn back." And they plodded on.

They followed the road round a bend and the next house came in view. It was larger than all the rest. Light poured out through the tall windows. It had to be Teddy Bear's house.

The front door looked so forbidding that they were afraid to ring the bell. They walked round the house and knocked at the back door. A maid came to see who was there.

The beam of light from the open door pierced the dark garden. The smell of roast meat wafted out. Terror and Sophie blinked their eyes.

"Is Teddy Bear at home?" asked Sophie.

"You must mean Mr Bear," said the maid. "And what do the likes of you want with the master? Be off with you, and be quick about it! We can do without beggars here." And bang! The kitchen door was slammed in their faces.

They walked back to the front of the house. The windows were set so high in the wall that they couldn't see inside. Terror jumped up on to a window ledge and pressed his nose against the glass. Sophie stood a few paces back. "What can you see?" she asked.

It began to snow. First a few small flakes, like little speckles dancing in the light. It wasn't sleet any more. Quickly the flakes grew bigger, and came whirling chaotically down. The garden turned white.

"They're playing about with gold and silver paper," said Terror.

"Who?"

"The Bear children. Mrs Bear is polishing apples with a cloth. Teddy Bear himself is sitting by the fire reading a newspaper. There's a Christmas tree, and the table is covered with tinsel and baubles and candles. The angel is already up on the top of the tree. They're putting sweets and nuts into little baskets . . ."

Sophie was stiff with cold. Snowflakes fell on her head and on her shoulders and settled there without melting away. She could no longer talk, her tongue and her lips were so stiff. The snow clung to her cheeks, to her front and to her legs. Before very long she was covered with a layer of snow from head to toe.

"They've got beautiful toys, Teddy Bear's children," said Terror. "They're drinking tea and eating raisins and pretzels and mandarins. They're singing Christmas carols. They're very sweet children, I must say . . ."

Then one of the children saw Terror sitting outside on the window ledge. "Mummy!" he shouted. "There's a cat outside the window!"

They all came up to the window to have a look at Terror.

"And just look over there!" they called out when they saw Sophie. "A snowman! Oh, oh, it's been snowing. Oh, please, please, may we go out?"

Sophie was frozen solid. Stock-still and white all over, she stood there in the beautiful white garden of Bear House.

After they'd put on their caps and scarves, the children rushed outside. Merrily they tumbled about in the snow and had a snowball fight. Teddy Bear and his wife looked on smiling.

The children also threw some snowballs at the snowman. Sophie, frozen stiff, wobbled a few times and then fell over.

The children bounded up to the over-turned snowman. One wanted to pull it up again, another wanted to tug the head from the body, but the third called out: "Bare feet! A snowman with bare feet!"

They had never seen a snowman like that before.

Teddy Bear and Mrs Bear came to have a look. Terror jumped down from the window ledge and joined them. He and Teddy Bear carried Sophie inside.

The servants were set to work. They lit a big fire in one of the bedrooms, carried in a tub of hot water and put at least twenty hot-water bottles in the bed.

Sophie's arms and legs were as stiff as planks. She was lowered into the hot bath and all the snow melted. Mrs Bear rubbed her dry with an enormous towel. Then they laid her in the bed and went away.

Terror was the only one to stay in the bedroom. He jumped up on to the bed and licked Sophie's face. He licked and licked

her until she opened her eyes and smiled at him. Then he went and lay down on her feet and pretended to be asleep.

It took a whole week for Sophie to thaw out completely and be allowed out of bed.

That marked the beginning of a glorious time for her. All day long she played with Teddy Bear's children. They would play hide-and-seek in the big house, race their sledges down a slope in the park, and tease the maids and footmen. They also made up little plays and performed them for Teddy Bear, Mrs Bear and Terror. Sometimes they went on trips in a sleigh drawn by two horses, visiting the families of friends in the district. Every night before they went to bed they got a mug of hot chocolate and a currant bun, and Mrs Bear read them fairy tales.

Sophie had even been given a toy of her own, a worn-out old teddy bear that the Bear children had no use for any more. She called him Pinky Bear. At night Pinky Bear and Ulliput slept next to her in bed, so that she never felt lonely.

Terror liked it in Teddy Bear's house as well. What he liked best was to sit in the library. All along the walls were bookcases full of books right up to the ceiling. Teddy Bear had never opened any of the books but he was happy to have a guest for once who was interested in them. Sometimes, too, to do Teddy Bear a favour, Terror would go with him to the stables to look at Teddy Bear's horses.

And they would sit together for hours in front of the fire discussing all the things that were wrong with the world. Terror would speak of the play he wanted to write and

Teddy Bear would tell racy stories. Most of these were about hunting parties or important friends of his who had had the most extraordinary adventures. Or he spoke of the journeys he would have made if he hadn't had so many things to do that kept him at home.

More than once, too, Teddy Bear and Terror would sit in the library, each in an easy chair on either side of the fire, and say nothing at all. Then thick clouds of blue cigar smoke would waft around the room, and Teddy Bear would refill the glasses or draw the cork from the next bottle. It was a very hospitable place, the Bear family's house.

Mrs Bear taught Sophie to knit, something all girls ought to know how to do, she thought. And Sophie knitted with a will, clicking away merrily with her needles as she turned out lots of little scarves and tiny caps, one after the other.

"Well now, dear child, have you made a scarf and a cap for every doll in the house yet?" Teddy Bear asked one day.

They had just sat down at the table. After the soup they had roast boar with currant jelly, baked potatoes, stuffed peppers and little broad beans as soft as butter.

Sophie blushed. "The little caps and scarves are not for the dolls," she said. "I've made them for . . . for the knob on the front door. Because it's cold! And for the knob on the back door, and the one on the stable door. That one's the coldest of all . . . Now I'm knitting for the spikes on the gate."

The whole family burst out laughing. Teddy Bear laughed with a deep rumbling sound, Mrs Bear gurgled, the little Bears shouted, and Terror sat there grinning. Even the maid who was just setting clean plates in front of them couldn't help laughing and ran out of the room. Sophie clapped Pinky Bear and Ulliput to her face so as not to show how embarrassed she was. And then she lost her temper.

"I'll have finished as soon as the spikes on the gate have got their caps," she cried. "Then no one will be cold any more! You don't know what cold is!" Her voice grew louder and louder.

"You've never been really cold!" she shouted, "what with your lovely house and your stoves and your fireplace! And all that food! Always eating and eating until you're sick to your stomachs! And . . . and . . .!" She almost choked with fury. "Oh," she exclaimed, "oh, Lanky Flop! I haven't thought of you at all lately!"

She burst into sobs. So upset was she that they had to carry her to bed.

That night Sophie had a horrible dream. She dreamt of Lanky Flop. He was sitting in his cell and the rats had eaten his feet and also a bit of his legs. She woke up, tossed and turned and fell asleep again.

Once again she dreamt. Now Lanky Flop was standing with his face turned towards the little grille above his cell door. Teasingly the guards were holding plates of the most tempting foods under his nose: roast meat, baked potatoes and beans soft as butter. Lanky Flop could smell it all, his mouth watering and his stomach contracting so tightly that he could have screamed with pain.

And Sophie herself woke up with a scream. Again she fell asleep. This time she dreamt that she was in a square, the self-same square in which she had lost her hair. There was no fair this time and yet there were crowds of people. In the middle of the square they had put up a gallows with a rope dangling from it. She couldn't see Lanky Flop.

When she woke up once more she was so sad that she couldn't fall asleep again. Softly she stole downstairs. Terror and Teddy Bear were sitting in the library, with glasses of ruby port in front of them.

"Look who's here!" said Teddy Bear. "Couldn't you sleep, little one?"

"No," said Sophie, "I must tell you something. We are . . . that is, Terror and I are . . . Lanky Flop is in prison! And the guard . . . we have to have some money!" She couldn't get her words out properly.

Teddy Bear sat, fiddling impatiently with his cigar, and that made Sophie cross. Words tumbling over each other, she told

him everything. "And so you'll have to give us five hundred guilders," she finished.

Terror nodded and said: "Yes, five hundred guilders should be just about enough to do it."

Teddy Bear paced up and down the room deep in thought.

"Well," he said at long last, "it's an excellent plan, a very good plan indeed. The only question is, will it work? One guard won't be able to do it on his own. The others will have to be bought off, as well. And even then . . . how will our friend make his getaway? By ship, by train, on foot, on horseback? For that he will need more help and more money.

"And what if they catch him again? He'll be guarded even more closely then. That would mean still more bribes . . . for the judge, the priest, the chief of police . . . I know them all, there's nothing you can tell me about them. No, my friends, it just won't work. I don't have that sort of money."

"Teddy Bear," said Sophie, "Teddy Bear, just listen. It's Lanky Flop we're talking about. You could sell your house, couldn't you, and all your belongings? You've got furniture, horses, a carriage . . . they all add up to a lot of money. There's no alternative. It's for Lanky Flop. He saved your life when you were sinking in the bog. Don't you think it's wonderful to have this opportunity to repay him?"

"Repay him?" said Teddy Bear. "Yes, yes, of course. I'd do anything for our friend. You have to believe me, little Sophie. He saved my life, as you say. Yes he did, he did indeed, but not the lives of Mrs Bear and all the Bear children. He didn't save their lives.

"So how can I possibly deprive them of their home and possessions? Leave them in poverty? That wouldn't be right, would it? No, no, we'll have to think of something else."

Again Teddy Bear walked up and down the room deep in thought. Terror and Sophie looked at each other. Terror had narrowed his eyes to slits, as if he were winking with both eyes at once. Sophie felt desperately sad. It was almost too late to save Lanky Flop, she thought, and it was all her fault.

"I've got it!" Teddy Bear suddenly shouted. He banged his head with his fist, so delighted was he that he had hit on such a brilliant idea.

"The king!" he said. "We'll get him to help us. He is sensible and has a kind heart, otherwise he wouldn't be king. And he has money to spare. A few thousand more or less wouldn't make any difference to him!"

The Dinner

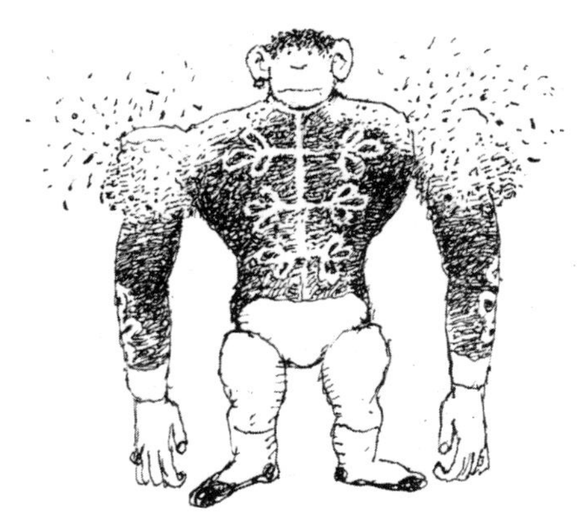

You may make all sorts of wonderful plans at night, but when the cold light of day falls on the breakfast table next morning very little of those plans remains as a rule. And that's what happened to Teddy Bear's plan.

"Kings don't much care for beggars," he explained.

"You promised," said Sophie. "You promised you would take us to the king. I'd like to talk to him. He has a kind heart and lots of money, you said so yourself."

"True enough," said Teddy Bear, "but in this country there's a law against begging, which is just as well. And if you appear before the king and ask him for money, you'll be a beggar and that's a punishable offence. I've got to give a little bit of thought to myself and my family, you know."

"And to Lanky Flop, we've got to give thought to him most of all," Sophie said. "All right then, I shan't ask him for any money, I'll just ask him to let Lanky Flop go. The king can do that, surely."

Teddy Bear looked worried. Mrs Bear couldn't see what the problem was. She nodded to Teddy Bear and said: "Dear husband, I do think we ought to help the child. She's worried about her friend, and that's nice of her. Couldn't you consult one of your friends at court?"

"Yes, yes, perhaps that would be the best thing to do." Teddy Bear was thinking. Then his face lit up. "Tonight the king is giving a dinner," he said. "It's Wednesday, and on Wednesdays he always gives a dinner. The most important people in the land are invited to go and eat with him. I know somebody who's been asked. That's who we'll go to for advice about what Sophie ought to do for the best."

"There you are! I was sure you'd find a solution," said Mrs Bear and smiled at her husband. "You are much too modest. As if you didn't have friends in the highest circles!"

That same afternoon Terror, Sophie and Teddy Bear drove in the carriage into town. They got out in front of a house in a narrow street. A lantern giving out a reddish glow hung above the door.

Although it was not yet completely dark, the curtains were drawn across every window. Teddy Bear rang the door bell.

A tall, broad-shouldered man with the battered face of a boxer opened the door. Sophie looked up at him nervously. Teddy Bear whispered something into the man's ear.

"Is that somebody from the highest circles, do you think?" Sophie asked Terror.

"Certainly not, he's the doorman," said Terror. "Just go along now with Teddy Bear and do your best. I'll wait for you outside and keep a good look out."

Inside the house everything was wonderfully elegant. There were carved and gilded chairs and tables everywhere and so many table lights that it might have been a lamp shop. There were palms in pots, and the floors and the staircase were covered with a thick red carpet. Sophie immediately felt at home in this lovely house.

Teddy Bear took her upstairs to one of the rooms. This was even more beautiful than the rest of the house. Wherever Sophie looked, she could see herself and Teddy Bear because of all the mirrors on the walls and even on the ceiling. She lost count of how many there were. In the middle of the

room stood a huge bed covered with satin cushions.

They didn't have long to wait. The door flew open and there stood . . . Annabella! She ran up to Sophie with a beaming smile, gave her a kiss and made her sit down on a low stool. Then she embraced Teddy Bear. She embraced him long and tenderly, as old friends do who have known each other for a long time.

Annabella and Teddy Bear sat down to talk. They talked so softly that Sophie couldn't hear them. Now and then Annabella would look over Teddy Bear's shoulder at Sophie and smile at her, or give her a wink.

"All right then, that's agreed," Teddy Bear said at long last, getting up and straightening his coat. "I'll have to be off now. You'll let me know how it goes, won't you?"

Sophie and Annabella were left alone. They sat and looked at each other and every so often Annabella burst out laughing. Sophie had no idea why.

"How nice your hair looks," said Annabella. "Much prettier than that spiky hair you used to have. Have you been to the hairdresser's, then?"

"No," said Sophie. "Did Teddy Bear tell you what happened to Lanky Flop? He said that someone here could take me to the king. So I could ask him to let Lanky Flop go free. Annabella . . . do you still remember . . . when we were travelling through the countryside and came to that bog? Lanky Flop was your friend, too, wasn't he?"

"Of course!" Annabella said. "What a character – but as poor as a church mouse, more's the pity. Tonight the two of us shall go to see the king. We'll put our best foot forward, as they say. You'll have to do all the talking. You are a respectable girl, he'll listen to you. He'll have to, he's the king. And if it's no good, at least we'll have had a good laugh. I'm always game for a laugh."

"Is it you who are going to dine with the king?" Sophie asked, taken aback. Annabella laughed.

"Don't look so worried, Sophie! Those people in the palace won't eat you, you know!"

Annabella and Sophie were let in through the back door of the palace. Sophie looked back once more; Terror and Teddy Bear were nowhere to be seen.

In the palace there were five different kitchens: one for roasting sheep and oxen on the spit, one for baking bread and pies, one where the soups were prepared, one for the vegetables and the other dishes, and one where the food was arranged beautifully on the platters before being carried through into the dining-room.

They were taken through to the bakery. Here the cooks were busy decorating huge whipped-cream cakes with sweetmeats and fruit. A few were baking pies stuffed with pigeon, quail and larks' tongues.

In the middle of the kitchen stood a long narrow table covered with a white cloth that

hung down to the floor. Three dome-shaped silver dish covers as large as church bells were on the table. Annabella had pushed Sophie under the tablecloth even before she had had a proper chance to look round. Annabella crept under the cloth too.

"We'll have ourselves carried to the king," she whispered to Sophie. "Then we'll suddenly come out and give the king and his guests a surprise. That's what the king likes. A sort of joke, you see?"

"But will I be able to talk to him?" said Sophie.

"Of course, don't be silly," said Annabella. "Look, that's where you've got to hide. You didn't imagine, surely, that someone like you could just walk straight into the king's room?"

A sort of bench had been slung under two of the silver covers, where two round holes had been cut in the table. Sophie had to sit on one of the benches. Filled with anxiety she doubled herself up, and sat with her head and shoulders inside the dish cover.

"Once we're there," whispered Annabella, "the Master of Ceremonies will take the cover off and then you'll have to be quick standing up. There'll be no need to be frightened, because you won't have to do anything else. I'll be under the cover at the other end. There's a cake under the middle one. Good fun, huh?"

"I don't think it's fun at all. All I want to do is talk to the king," said Sophie.

"Now look, for goodness' sake don't be so childish! Keep still, all right? Here we go then!"

Annabella disappeared and Sophie sat completely still on the little bench. She could see nothing with her head inside the dish cover, although she could hear the cooks talking and laughing. And she could hear Annabella's voice as well. Sophie's knees were beginning to ache from being doubled up for so long. "It's got to be done for Lanky Flop's sake," she said to herself. Her heart was in her mouth.

At long last Sophie felt the table being lifted and carried away. She had to hold on tight so as not to fall off her little perch. In the distance she could hear violins and flutes and drums. The music came steadily closer and closer.

The king and his guests had eaten and drunk so much that they had nearly burst. The king sat at one end of the table and the queen sat at the other. They couldn't talk to each other because of the distance between them. To the left of the king sat his most important guests, to his right those who were less important. On a platform an orchestra was playing.

The king was tired out from all the eating and drinking. His stomach was much too full, and he felt very uncomfortable. He would have loved to have had a snooze. But every time he leant back a little and began to nod off he could feel the queen giving him a piercing look from a distance, and he would wake again with a start. Then he'd immediately put on a face as if he'd all along been sitting there enjoying the music. The king was a great lover of music. He began to hum the melody. Suddenly he bellowed: "What the devil is going on? Someone is out of tune again! It's the second fiddle! Away with him!"

The music didn't miss a beat. The members of the orchestra tried even harder to play better than before. They didn't seem to turn a hair. And yet they could see perfectly well that a soldier was dragging the second violinist off. And they knew that the poor fellow's life wasn't worth a bean. He would be thrown into jail and next morning at dawn he would be executed.

The king was quite unable to keep in tune himself. The musicians never knew which of them would be accused by him of playing the wrong note. Or the wrong beat, for that was something else he watched. He would tap his foot along with the music. And he couldn't keep time either.

"What the devil!" yelled the king. "The drummer is drumming out of time! That's the last straw!"

And the drummer too was dragged off. There was a great shortage of musicians in the country.

The guests were sleepy. They had drunk much too much wine. But when the Master

of Ceremonies announced the dessert, they woke up again, for when it was time for dessert they could always count on a surprise. Like a spouting fountain that showered them with champagne, or a huge bowl full of ice in all the colours of the rainbow, with living goldfish flopping about inside.

The least important guests, those who sat to the king's right, had to get up and move their chairs back. Scores of footmen rushed to and fro. The dining-room table was pushed against a wall and the table with the three dish covers put in its place. The least important guests were allowed to draw their chairs up to the table again.

First the middle cover was raised. The guests all called out: "Brilliant! Delicious! Superb!" and clapped their hands. They would never have let on that they were

disappointed to find it was only a common or garden whipped-cream cake there on the table, even if it was big enough to feed a company of soldiers for a week.

The footmen handed round helpings of cake. When everyone had been given a piece, the other two covers were raised. The room fell completely quiet.

Sophie stood up at once, as arranged. She was too frightened to look up until suddenly she heard a deafening outburst of laughter and cheering. At first all she could see was Annabella, on the other side of the cream cake.

Annabella was naked except for a few little butterflies stuck here and there. The little butterflies sparkled, reflecting the light of the hundreds of candles.

Then Sophie saw the queen. She was staring at Annabella with disgust; then she rose to her feet and left the room with her nose in the air.

Sophie hardly dared look at all the gentlemen around the table in their uniforms bedecked with gold and silver stars and other decorations. To the left and right were wide-open laughing mouths, gold teeth, greasy whiskers, watering eyes and shiny red faces. And they were all pointing at her.

Timidly she turned round and then she saw the king. He had almost fainted with laughter. He was clutching his fat stomach with both hands. He hiccupped, roared, squeezed his eyes shut, howled, stared at Sophie and then picked up the first thing he could lay his hands on, a cherry, and flung it at her. The cherry hit Sophie on her tummy and stuck to her nightdress.

Sophie forgot where she was. She no longer remembered that she had come to the king's palace to ask the king to let Lanky Flop go. She didn't even remember that it was the king who was laughing at her and who had thrown a mouldy cherry at her. She bent down, plunged both hands into the cream cake and hurled a huge blob of whipped cream into the king's face. The king sagged back in his chair and blinked his eyes, thickly smeared with whipped cream.

"Take that, and that, and that!" said Sophie, and with every "that!" she threw another handful of whipped cream without caring where it landed.

There was no more laughter and no more cheering. The dining-room was deathly quiet. Annabella, pale with fright, stared at the furious Sophie. Annabella could have been a statue, one hand at her mouth and the other pressed to one of the glittering butterflies. Her eyes grew rounder and rounder. Then suddenly she began to shout with happy laughter, bursting with admiration for Sophie, the cream-thrower.

Four soldiers marched stiffly up to the table, seized hold of Sophie and carried her off.

The Trial

Sophie had been asleep. She was woken up by a rustling in the straw. Outside she could hear the heavy footsteps of the prison guard. There was no other sound.

High in the wall was a small barred window. Through the little window she could see a star glittering in the black night sky. Sometimes she thought the star had disappeared, for it twinkled as if it was being switched on and off. She lay there looking at the star and thought: "I have been dreaming. But what did I dream? Something very nice . . ." Try as she would she could not recall her dream, and yet it had given her a wonderfully peaceful feeling.

Sophie knew that all was lost now. She had ruined everything. There was no hope left for Lanky Flop and things looked just as bad for her. But she was not afraid. She even felt quite cheerful. She thought that was odd, and couldn't work out how it came about.

In the next cell somebody started to sing:

"Have some pity, pity, Hetty!
Is there no room left for me?
Pushed against this iron frame
In a trice I'll fall again!
Tralala and tralalee!"

In less than a trice Sophie was standing with her ear pressed to the wall. She knew that voice so well! Lanky Flop was in the cell next door and he was singing!

She knocked on the wall. But Lanky Flop couldn't hear her because he had started to whistle the same tune.

"Silence!" roared the guard. "Prisoners are forbidden to whistle or to sing."

"Quite right, too," said Lanky Flop, "and laughing is forbidden here too. Would you like me to whimper a bit?"

All was silent again. Trembling all over, Sophie was still standing by the wall. "I must let Lanky Flop know I'm here," she thought. "I'd better sing something too. How did that song of his go again?"

She didn't know the tune and she had already forgotten the words. She'd just have to sing another song, one from the good old days.

Sophie sang:

"Swing up, swing down, swing high, swing low,
Higher and higher I will go.
Hold the ropes and hold them fast,
Like a sailor up the mast!"

"Sophie!!!" called Lanky Flop. "Sophie!!!"

"Silence!" roared the guard. "Prisoners are forbidden to speak to each other!"

Again the still of the night crept into the cell and with the silence a sense of solitude. Sophie put both her hands against the wall to be as close to Lanky Flop as possible. Like that she felt her way along the length of the wall until she was standing in the corner under the little window. She leant her head against the cold stone, and was startled. She could hear knocking on the other side of the wall. There was also a scrabbling sound and a little plaster fell off. She put her ear against the spot.

"Little Sophie!" she heard Lanky Flop whisper. "Little Sophie! Can you hear me?"

There was a small hole in the wall. Quickly, Sophie put her mouth against it and said softly: "I can hear you very well. You were blowing right in my ear! Now say something else, while I put my ear to the hole again."

They talked and talked, so long that the star disappeared and the sky took on colour and grew light without their noticing. Lanky Flop explained that he had made the hole in the wall with a piece of metal he had found under the floor of his cell. The cell next to his had been empty for a long time, but last night he had heard that a new prisoner was expected. He hadn't known who that was, and that's why he had started to sing, in the hope of getting an answer.

"Now tell me everything that's happened to you and how you got here! Did you do something wrong? Don't tell me you stole something?" he asked.

Sophie told Lanky Flop everything. She confessed that for a time at the beginning she hadn't given him any thought and that she was very sorry about that. She told him about the dinner at the king's palace and what had happened there. As Sophie told her tale, Lanky Flop had great difficulty in not bursting out laughing.

"Oh, oh, that Annabella!" he said. "What a fantastic woman she is. And what about Teddy Bear? Shall I tell you something, little Sophie? People who are loaded like that are hopeless cases, much worse off than we are. They've got no backbone at all and if you take all their possessions away from them they're completely done for."

"But *we* are done for this time," said Sophie.

"Not quite, my girl. I'm not allowing my head to drop that quickly. Even if the rest of me is going to hang. Now, now, don't cry!"

"And I don't know where Terror is, either," Sophie sobbed softly.

"Have you still got that silly doll with you?" asked Lanky Flop, to distract her a bit.

"No," sobbed Sophie, "I forgot to bring Ulliput and Pinky Bear as well. I am all alone."

"Lucky you've still got me, then," said Lanky Flop. "Sing me that little song again. I never knew you were such a good singer."

Sophie knew perfectly well that Lanky Flop was just saying that to cheer her up. He didn't much care for crying girls. She wanted very much to please him, but she was so tired from all that had been happening that she couldn't remember a single song properly.

With her mouth to the hole in the cell wall, she sang softly:

"Have pity, have pity,
On me in my bed,
In my great iron bed,
Ulliput's fallen over the edge,
Pinky Bear, Pinky Bear's gone up so fast,
Like a sailor he's gone up the mast."

It wasn't a happy song. Even Lanky Flop, on the other side of the wall, felt his knees go weak, and his eyes filled with tears.

"Don't be so sad," he whispered in Sophie's ear.

"I'm not sad," Sophie whispered back. "With you as my friend, I'm not sad."

It was the last thing they had time to say to each other.

Soldiers marched into the cell, followed by the prison governor and the head of police. Sophie's hands were tied behind her back with a stout rope. Then they took her outside and there was Lanky Flop, with his hands tied behind his back too. They weren't able to say anything to each other. With soldiers on either side of them, they were marched in procession to the market square.

So many people were about that Sophie didn't at first notice the platform that had been put up on one side of the square. Under a canopy, decked with golden tassels and bunting, a throne had been placed for the king. Trumpets blared and drums rolled.

"Long live the king! Long live the king!" people shouted from all sides.

Stiff-legged, the king, followed by his ministers and chamberlains, strutted to his throne. Sophie could not believe her eyes when she saw who was walking arm in arm with the king. It wasn't the queen – it was Annabella! She was swaying her hips and laughing merrily.

Not once did she look at the two prisoners who, ringed round by soldiers armed to the teeth, stood facing the platform. She never even saw them. She had eyes only for the king and was busy doing all she could to please him. She lifted his coat as he climbed the few steps to his throne so that he didn't stumble, she adjusted his sash and straightened his wig, which had slipped down over one of his ears.

"Ahem, ahem," Lanky Flop said, and Sophie realised that there was something else to be seen.

She followed Lanky Flop's glance and found Terror, not far from them. He, too, pretended he had nothing to do with them. And then she spotted Teddy Bear; he was walking in the retinue close behind the king, and took a chair at the end of a row. He, too, did not look at the prisoners, but carried on a conversation with the important personage sitting next to him.

The trial began. Lanky Flop was the first to be called forward. The prosecutor read the indictment: "The accused, Lanky Flop by name, born in such and such a place on such and such a date, resident in such and

such a town, etcetera, etcetera, stands accused of theft: a golden watch together with a golden watch chain; by snatching the above-named objects from the hand of their rightful owner So-and-so, which event took place on such and such a day of the year of our Lord Such-and-such, as witness . . ."

It was a very long recital.

"Accused," said the judge, "do you plead guilty to the charge?"

Lanky Flop held his head to one side and reflected for a moment. "Plead guilty to the charge?" he said. "If I do, I'll have had it for sure, but I must say, and I'll tell you this straight, and it's from the heart, that I think the indictment is a wonderfully clever piece of writing – how that fellow thought it all out, he must have had to go to school for years and years and years to come up with something like that – I could never have told it so cleverly myself, but whether it all happened exactly as that fellow says, well, now, look here, it was all a long time ago and my memory is not so good, what with all the time I've been in prison . . ."

The king was standing up. "Hold your tongue!!" his voice thundered across the market square. "Impudent scoundrel! Noose!" And he made an elegant gesture with his hand as if knotting a rope at the side of his head.

The people, who had been standing packed together and listening in silence, now cried "Aaaah!" with one voice, and all heads turned from the king to the accused as if a gust of wind had swept through a willow-grove.

"Next!" the prosecutor called. The soldiers pushed Sophie forward.

Only then did the king see Sophie. He stared at her, his mouth dropped open, and he blinked his eyes as if he could still feel the thick whipped cream she had thrown in his face. He stretched out his arm, pointed and stammered: "That . . . that . . . this . . . that . . .!" Then, deathly pale, he collapsed on to his throne.

Now Annabella sprang into action. She brought out a little flask, and everyone watching her assumed that she was holding smelling salts under the king's nose, a remedy for bringing people round who are feeling faint. In fact she had put something quite different into the little flask: a soporific potion. The king fell at once into a deep sleep.

No one could see exactly what was happening, or come near the king, because Annabella had hidden him from view behind her wide skirts. Then she suddenly started to shriek and to wail: "Help! Help! What are you all doing just standing there day-dreaming! The poor king! Oh! Oh! He's dying! Our king is passing away!"

Then all the important gentlemen sitting on the platform, together with the judge and the prosecutor and many, many more, rushed to the king's aid. They paid no attention to Annabella. Bending down, she had vanished in no time at all between the legs of the crowd.

The soldiers stood on tiptoe, craning their necks to look over the heads of those in front of them. They forgot all about their duty to guard the prisoners. All the people in the market square were crowding to the front, almost flattening each other and treading on a lot of toes. The throng was so great that some were even pushed down the well and one boy was wrapped round a lamp-post like a snake.

Sophie and Lanky Flop suddenly felt their ropes being cut. "Quick! Quick! Follow us!" someone whispered. There was Annabella, with a knife in her hand. Terror was there too. They were being so tightly pressed

against Lanky Flop and Sophie that the two of them almost disappeared into Terror's fur and Annabella's clothes.

Terror went first. Swiftly he slipped between the people who were still pushing and shoving and cursing to get closer to the king.

At one point they heard someone call: "Hey! Hey! Where are you going?" They paid no attention, and it was only after they had raced through a number of streets that they realised that it was Teddy Bear who was following behind them.

As soon as it became clear that the king wasn't dead and that the prisoners had made good their escape, the crowd in the market square turned as one man and started to chase them. They could hear hundreds of feet running behind them.

"Oh dear, oh dear!" cried Annabella. "I've got a stitch in my side!"

"Faster, faster!" hissed Terror.

"They won't catch me!" called Lanky Flop.

And Teddy Bear growled: "We're going as fast as we can."

Sophie said nothing; she needed all her breath to carry on running.

"There they are!" she heard someone shout. "The girl is there too!"

"Hurry up!" called Terror, shooting past them like a rocket, and rushing on to the quay and up a gangplank.

They ran after him across the wobbly plank and on to the deck of a ship where they landed, still running, so that they fell all over each other because they could go no farther. Terror pulled up the gangplank, cast off and took the helm.

The sails had already been hoisted and they puffed out in the stiff westerly breeze. A pennant fluttered from the top of the mast. The little ship rocked as it swept out of the harbour, bobbing up and down in the waves. And so it reached the open sea and set course for the horizon.

The Storm

The night was bright. Thousands of stars lit up the sky and the moon slipped across from left to right. Deep in thought, Teddy Bear walked across the deck with his hands clasped behind his back. Lanky Flop, Annabella and Sophie were asleep. Terror was at the helm and was keeping watch.

Early in the morning the wind began to pick up. The sun hid away behind grey clouds. "Heavy weather on its way," Terror said, and took in all but one of the sails.

The clouds climbed high, towering on top of each other in dark piles. By midday, the wind was howling through the rigging, battering the little ship to and fro and whipping up the waves, which foamed upwards, swirled, curled over and came crashing down like waterfalls.

"You must lash yourselves to something quickly!" shouted Terror. "There's some rope over there, tie yourselves to the mast or else you'll be washed overboard!"

Scarcely had he spoken when the first heavy sea broke over the deck, soaking the fugitives to the skin. Shivering with fear and cold they huddled together under the mast. There was no time to tie themselves to anything before the ship had been suddenly lifted up on high and smashed down again like a helpless toy. There was a loud crack, and with a thunderous roar the mizzen-mast plunged into the sea, snapped off like a matchstick. The yards and the rigging were left hanging overboard, and the ship began listing dangerously to one side.

Teddy Bear wailed: "Oh, why did I have to come along? Ah, my darling wife, dearest Mrs Bear, forgive your loving husband! From now on I shall always stay faithfully at home, if I'm saved, that is, and never listen to strange women again. Ah, my dear little wife, our last hour has struck!" And he shut his eyes tightly so that he would no longer have to see the terrifying ocean with its pounding waves.

"We could do without that sort of nincompoop," Annabella said. "Let's get a move on, Lanky Flop darling, or do you want to drown too?" So saying, she made for the wheelhouse, picked up an axe and began to hack furiously at the ropes attached to the broken-off end of the mast. The weight of the mast was making the boat lurch more and more to port.

Roughly Lanky Flop pushed her to one side, seized the axe out of her hand and began hitting the rigging with powerful blows. Splinters of wood flew about his ears. "Hold tight! Hold tight!" he shouted.

For the second time a heavy sea broke over the deck.

For a few moments nothing at all could be seen of the ship. They all lay where they had been flung on the deck. Water was everywhere all round them. They could feel fish and jellyfish brushing past their faces. But a moment later the bowsprit was pointing upwards again and the ship quivered

and heaved and shook off the water like a wet dog.

Meanwhile Sophie had found a knife in the wheelhouse. She wanted to use it to help cut through the ropes, but first she had to disentangle a starfish that had been stranded in her hair, since the poor creature would be better off in the sea.

No one had time to look at anyone else, which was probably just as well. Terror had the appearance of a drowned water-rat, a skinny little animal with soaking fur. And Annabella, whose clothes were clinging to her body, had hair so wet and full of seaweed that she could have been a Fury or a water nymph. Lanky Flop looked as thin as a lead pencil. He was still hitting away furiously with the axe. After yet another crashing blow, which succeeded in smashing the rails to pieces as well, the mast disappeared beneath the waves. Slowly the ship righted itself. The greatest danger had passed.

Teddy Bear had not even noticed how bravely his friends had stood up to the ordeal. Like a woebegone bundle of misery he sat crumpled up in a corner. He couldn't even summon up the spirit to wail any more. He looked up only when he heard Lanky Flop call out: "The worst is over! Chin up, Sophie! It's all going to turn out for the best, Annabella, my love!"

At that very moment a flash of lightning shot straight out of the black sky into the waves, followed immediately by a booming clap of thunder. Another flash of lightning! Everywhere they looked around the little ship lightning was striking the sea. The crashing of the thunder drowned out the roar of the wind.

Then they heard an awful howl. It was the kind of howl only tomcats could make. Terror, who had remained calm throughout all their tribulations, was standing now by the helm with his lips snarling, showing his white teeth. His ears were lying flat against his head. Desperately he was pulling at the wheel, which was spinning round and round like a top.

"We're done for!" he shouted. "The rudder's fouled!"

The others crawled towards him on their hands and knees for fear of being blown overboard. "What's happened?" they asked.

"I don't know!" cried Terror in despair. "The rudder doesn't respond any more. And visibility is so poor that we could hit a reef at any moment."

Now the danger was greater than ever. They could see barely ten yards ahead through the towering waves. Terrified, they stood closely together, clinging to one another, awaiting the impact of a collision if the ship were to run on to rocks.

"One of us will have to get up the foremast to act as a lookout and sound the alarm," said Terror. "As soon as the alarm is given, we'll all have to jump overboard. Then you'll have to try to grab hold of a piece of wreckage to hang on to . . ."

"Why should anyone have to do anything so risky?" asked Lanky Flop. "You can't see any farther up there than down here. And if we hit a reef you could shout as hard as you liked up there – no one down here would hear a thing."

Annabella seemed the least frightened of all. "I'll go up," she said with a beaming face. She gave one of her happy, gurgling little laughs.

"No, in no circumstances," said Lanky Flop. "You're so smooth and slippery, there's no way you'd be able to get up the mast."

Sophie had been listening without saying anything. Suddenly her mind was made up; before the rest could notice she had stolen

away. Holding on tight to whatever she could, she reached the mast and began to climb.

She climbed and she climbed. The mast swayed to and fro, making her dizzy. The higher she climbed, the more the mast swayed backwards and forwards, and from left to right, but to her surprise her giddiness disappeared again. She felt both a wonderful calmness and excitement. She did not give a thought to the danger she was in.

Sophie climbed to the very top of the mast, brushed her wet hair out of her face, opened her eyes wide and looked around.

"How beautiful the world is!" she cried. "How marvellous everything is, and so . . . so . . . oh, I don't know what. Oh, oh, what waves! I'm so happy! So happy!"

The waves were so high that they hid the horizon. They were green and white and black and above them the clouds tore by in all shades of grey. Everything was moving. Flashes of lightning, blue and yellow, lit up the sea and the sky over and over again. Everything would become bright then and for a moment it would look as if another, completely new, world had taken the place of the old familiar one.

The rain beat the deck with the sound of a hundred drums, and the wind whistled in the rigging. Sophie felt as if she were dancing and whirling to the sound of wild music.

And she was whirling – the whole ship was turning. The mast, with Sophie on it, turned round too. At first the ship followed a wide circle, but that didn't last long. Then she saw that a twirling hole had appeared in the water that was turning faster and faster in smaller and smaller circles towards the middle. "A whirlpool!" she shouted, but no one heard her.

The little ship flew round and round, coming closer and closer in towards the middle . . .

Everything on deck that had not been made properly fast vanished over the rails. A coil of rope, a crate, an oil drum, a coffee can, a box of ship's biscuits, everything flew overboard and joined in the twirling dance of the waves.

"Ulliput!" cried Sophie, as she saw her little doll follow a large wicker bottle through the air and disappear in the furious waves. Sophie peered and peered but there was no trace of the little doll. Loudly she began to sing:

"Ulliput's fallen over the edge,
Pinky Bear, Pinky Bear's gone up so fast,
Like a sailor he's gone up the mast!"

She looked around carefully and a moment later she discovered Pinky Bear. The wind and the twirling movement of the ship had indeed flung him high up into the mast's rigging, where he was dangling.

Brightly Sophie sang:

"Have pity, have pity,
on me in my bed,
in my great iron bed . . ."

Then she couldn't sing any more. The ship had come to the middle of the whirlpool and was turning and turning like a top at a frenzied speed. Sophie wasn't giddy yet, but she closed her eyes tight and let herself go round and round, and she whispered with a laugh: "Oh, what a lot of things life has to offer! That's what I wanted to find out. What a lot! What a lot!"

CRASH!

There they stood: Lanky Flop, Teddy Bear, Terror and Annabella. The cloth at the back of the stage had been fully wound across from one side to the other – there was nothing left on the right-hand pole and there was a fat roll round the left-hand pole. Painted on the piece of cloth in between were clouds, rain clouds. Nothing else. And in front of the cloth, on the floor, lay Sophie.

The room had been carefully tidied up. All the dolls and toy animals were back in their places, on top of the chest or in the drawers, just where they belonged. Only August the Clown was still out. He was standing with his arms folded, waiting impatiently.

"Well, that certainly didn't go according to plan," he said. "And that one there doesn't belong here because she didn't start out with the rest of you. I can't imagine how that came about." He pointed to Annabella. "And what happened to her?" he asked, nudging Sophie with his foot. She lay motionless on the stage, eyes shut.

"It's all over," Terror said. "You can go now."

"Well, if you don't need me any more . . ." said August the Clown. He pulled a face that was haughty and offended at the same time. Stiffly he walked over to his place on the chest.

Annabella, Teddy Bear, Lanky Flop and Terror stood still and stared at Sophie. Lanky Flop shook his head. Then he bent down, gently lifted Sophie up and carried her to bed.

There were many, many visitors. All the neighbours and the whole family came to have a last look at the dead girl. They all brought flowers for her. Mr Jerome came as well. He sobbed like a child and placed a bunch of forget-me-nots at her feet.

Night fell. Candles burned in the room. Sophie's father and mother wanted to stay awake, but their eyes closed with weariness. Grief makes you very tired.

It was quiet in the house. It was quiet outside on the street, too. Terror pushed the door of the room open. He jumped up on to the bed, pushed the forget-me-nots to one side and lay down in his usual place at Sophie's feet. He shut his eyes tight and began to purr softly.

Lanky Flop sat on the floor leaning against a bedpost. He looked as if he was asleep, but he wasn't.

Very early in the morning, Terror jumped on to the window-sill and began to wash himself. The sun was not yet up and all the people were still asleep. Outside in the street the horn of a car sounded, twice. Toot! Toot! Terror looked out.

He turned and jumped back into the room. He woke up Lanky Flop, who had finally dozed off. They whispered together for a few moments.

Lanky Flop stretched, yawned and scratched his head. Bringing his face close to Sophie's ear he said very softly: "Little Sophie! Little Sophie!" and kissed her on her mouth.

Slowly Sophie sat up; she blinked her eyes.

"Come," said Lanky Flop. He took her hand and drew her to the window.

In front of the house stood a motorcar: the most beautiful motorcar there had ever been. It was coloured a deep blue and it glittered in the first rays of the morning sun. Teddy Bear stood waiting beside it; impatiently he rocked to and fro on his heels or leaned against the car drumming his fingers on the gleaming paintwork. In the front, next to the driver's seat, sat Annabella. She looked up and waved.

Lanky Flop went out first, then came Sophie and Terror. They clambered through the window and climbed down the Russian vine that grew against the wall of the house.

"You three get in the back," said Teddy Bear, and revved the engine a little.

They drove through green hills and under blue skies. A warm breeze wafted the scent of a thousand flowers into their faces.

Teddy Bear turned the radio on. Annabella asked: "Anyone like a chocolate cream?" With their arms around one another they sat listening to the music and munching chocolates.

"Shall I tell you a joke?" Lanky Flop asked.

Sophie laughed. An endless journey was beginning.